2

True stories

Mike Samuda

Illustrated by
Peter Bowdler
Martin Cottam
Peter Dennis
Carol Hughes
Angela Maddigan
Stephen Morse
Paddy Mounter
Gary Rees
Ken Stott
Martin White
Paul Wright

Oxford University Press

Contents

The publishers would like to thank the following for permission to reproduce photographs:

Ardea Photographics, pp. 10, 11; Ardea/Ron and Valerie Taylor, p. 58; Anne Bolt, pp. 78, 79; J. Allan Cash, p. 84; Robert Harding, pp. 82, 86; H. J. Heinz Co. Ltd., p. 87; Judges Ltd., p. 99; Edward Leigh, p. 19; Mary Rose Trust, pp. 20, 21, 22, 23; National Film Board, Ottawa, p. 80; North Yorkshire Police, p. 97; James Robertson and Sons, p. 87; Royal Zoological Society of Ireland, p. 104; Syndication International, p. 111; John Topham, p. 85.

Oxford University Press 1980
Reprinted 1985, 1987
Printed in Hong Kong

Grandad's secret

Ian ran downstairs.
He was late for breakfast.
His sister was sitting at the table.
She had almost finished eating.

'Morning, sleepy head,' said Sally.
'Morning, Sal.
   Where's Gran?' asked Ian.
'She's making the sandwiches.
   Have you forgotten?
   We're going for a walk today.'
Sally covered her toast with jam.
'Nobody makes jam like Gran,' she said.
'Well, leave some for me,' said Ian.

Grandad came into the room.
He was wearing his old, flat hat
   and carrying his walking stick.
'Are you two ready?
   We'll leave by the back gate.'
He walked out to the garden.
He didn't wait for the two children.

Sally and Ian pulled on their anoraks.
They kissed Gran goodbye.
They ran into the garden.
Grandad was looking at his rabbits.
'Now that's a pair of rabbits,' he said.
   'Look at their magnificent coats.'
He pushed a carrot into the cage.
Then he went out through the back gate.
He started to walk up the road.

Sally looked at Ian.
'Why does he walk on his own?
   He never waits for us.'
Ian didn't say anything.
He liked his Grandad.
But he didn't know why.
Grandad was already a long way up the road
They raced after him.

They reached the top of a steep hill.
Grandad stopped and pulled out his pipe.
He smiled.
He came up here nearly every day.
It always made him feel good.
The old man pointed to a small wood.
'That's where we're going.
    We may see something wonderful.
    But don't ask me what.
    Just wait and see!'
He sucked on his pipe.
He smiled for the second time that day.

The old man walked off.
He started to sing.
Ian and Sally knew the song.
They both joined in.
  'Oh you'll never go to heaven,
  In an old Ford car.
  'Cos an old Ford car,
  Won't go that far.'
Three songs later they reached the wood.

'Right, no more noise,' said Grandad.
  'Just sit here and don't move.
  Eat your lunch.
  But remember, no talking.'
The time went by very slowly.

Ian and Sally soon finished their sandwiches.
There was nothing to do.
They watched their grandfather.
He was staring at the trees.

'Look!' said Grandad.
  'There's two of them.
  They're feeding by the rock.
  Can you see them?'
Ian looked at the rock.
There was nothing there.
But Sally saw something.
There were two brown shapes.
She stared very hard.
'Ian, it can't be true.
  Do you see what I see?'

Ian was puzzled.
There wasn't anything there.
Then something moved.
'I saw it!
   It hopped!
   There's another,' cried Ian.
He watched in silence for several minutes.
It was impossible.
He was in England watching two wallabies.
They were just like baby kangaroos.
He knew that wallabies only lived in Australia.

One of the wallabies stopped feeding.
It looked around.
It had heard something.
It jumped away into the woods.
The other followed a second later.

'They won't come back now.
 We've scared them away,' said Grandad.
'Now I want you to promise me something.
 Never tell anyone about the wallabies.
 Will you promise?'
Ian and Sally nodded.
They were still too surprised to talk very much.

It was getting late in the afternoon.
So they started the long walk back.
Sally was the first to speak.
'Grandad, why mustn't we talk about the wallabies?'
'They must be left alone,' said Grandad.
   'I don't want thousands of people looking for them.
   Wallabies are very shy animals.'

'Grandad's right,' said Ian.
   'But where do they come from?'
Grandad filled his pipe.
'There was a zoo near here.
   Two wallabies escaped.
   This was during the war.
   Somehow the wallabies got through
      the first winter.
   Now there are at least ten
      living around here.'

Sally and Ian's holiday was nearly over.
They went back to Manchester the next day.
They kept their promise.
They didn't even tell their Mum and Dad.

Of course you'd like to know where
   the wallabies live.
All I can tell you is this:
   the wallabies are very well.
An old man with a flat cap
   keeps an eye on them. . .
      somewhere in Derbyshire.

King Henry's great ship

It was a hot day in July, 1545.
England was at war with France.
A twelve-year-old boy was climbing a tall mast.
He didn't look down.
At last he reached the top.
Now he had a good view of the French ships.
He tried to count them.
But there were too many.
'French ships to the south,' yelled the boy.

He felt afraid.
The French ships were coming closer.
He heard a drum roll from below.
He looked down.
The deck was crowded with English soldiers.
There were five hundred men on the *Mary Rose*.
He wasn't alone.

He looked over to the English shore.
He saw the King's flag.
It was flying from Southsea Castle.
There were soldiers around the castle.
This was the main English army.
The boy looked for the King.
He saw a large man on horseback.
He was sure it was King Henry.

The French fired first.
The boy watched the smoke.
Then he saw the splashes in the water.
He waited for the *Mary Rose* to fire back.
Crash went the *Mary Rose*'s ninety-one guns.
The boy cheered as they went off.

King Henry VIII watched the battle.
He was pleased.
Everything was going well.
He saw the *Mary Rose* move forward.
No French ship was better than his battleship.
Then the King's face went white.
The *Mary Rose* was leaning over too far.
Water was pouring into the ship.
It rolled slowly over and began
   to disappear below the waves.
Two masts were left sticking out of the sea.
The huge battleship had sunk.

The young boy held on tight.
His feet were in the water.
Only the tip of the mast was above the waves.
Twenty sailors were saved from the *Mary Rose*.
The boy was one of them.

French soldiers landed on the south coast.
They were quickly pushed back into the sea.
They fled to their ships.
The ships returned to France.

King Henry had won.
But he had lost the *Mary Rose*.
The ship had been overloaded.
This one mistake killed hundreds of men.

The *Mary Rose* was forgotten.
She lay under eighteen metres of water.
Four hundred years went by.
In 1965 nobody knew exactly where she had sunk.
Then Alexander McKee read about the *Mary Rose*.
He wanted to find the great battleship.

The experts laughed at McKee.
They said that wooden ships break up under the sea.
'He might find a few guns.
  But he'll never find the *Mary Rose*.
  There isn't any ship left,' said one expert.

Mr. McKee didn't listen.
He read many books on the battle of 1545.
He studied hundreds of old maps.
He started searching in the muddy waters
    near Portsmouth.
He had friends who enjoyed underwater swimming.
They helped him with his search.
They found lots of rubbish, but no *Mary Rose*.

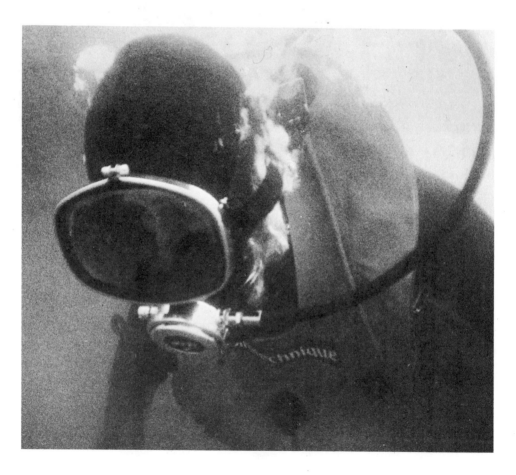

After a while McKee felt like giving up.
Then he had an idea.
Maybe the *Mary Rose* was under the mud.

'We need a special machine,' he told his friends.
   'It will show us if there's anything under the mud.
   It may help us find the ship.'
They used the machine very carefully.
There *was* something under the mud.
Was it the *Mary Rose*?
There was only one way to find out.
They started digging.

After months of work they found something.
It was a large lump of iron.
They cleaned it very carefully.
It was a gun.
The gun was from the *Mary Rose*.

The work went on.
It was difficult and very dirty.
At last they found some wood.
The wood seemed to be new.
It was tested by scientists.
They proved that the wood was
    four hundred years old.
It had been protected by the mud.

The remains of a wooden keg from the *Mary Rose*.

The diving became very exciting.
The divers could see the sides of the ship.
The battleship hadn't broken up after all.
The experts were wrong.
McKee was right.

There is a lot of work to do.
The problem is money.
It will cost thousands of pounds to uncover the ship.
McKee wants to bring the ship to the surface.
Maybe one day *we* will be able to see the *Mary Rose*.
The story of the *Mary Rose* has still not finished.

In the middle of the night

The only sound was the policeman's footsteps.
He shone his torch into the empty doorways.
The town clock chimed twice.
The policeman looked at his watch.
'Just three more hours,' said the policeman.
  'Then it's home to bed for me.'

He looked into the brightly-lit shop windows.
'Look at the price of that dress.
   Who can afford things like that?'
The policeman stared at one of the dummies
   in the window.
There was something wrong.
At first he didn't know what it was.
Then he laughed.
'They've put two right hands on that one
   in the red dress.
   Well done!' he said to himself.
   'What a detective I'll be one day.'

The policeman crossed the road.
He watched a motor-bike roar past.
It was going well over the speed limit.
'Still, I'm not going to throw myself
   in front of it.
   Now, down this alley, through the market,
      then round the back of the supermarket.
   What an exciting life I have!'

Then he heard the noise.
He stood perfectly still.
It was a dull, roaring noise.
It came from the supermarket car park.
He pulled out his radio.
'Blue Delta to Papa One.
    Do you read me, Papa One?'
A crackle came from his radio.
'This is Papa One.
    Report in, Blue Delta.'
The policeman whispered into the radio.
'Something is going on near the supermarket.
    I'm going to have a look.
    If it's anything serious I'll let you know.
    Over and out.'

He switched off the radio.
He pulled out his truncheon.
As he walked towards the supermarket
  the roaring noise became louder.

A high wall cut off his view of the car park.
Slowly he walked alongside the wall.
He kept in the dark shadow.
Carefully he climbed on to a large dustbin.
Now he could just see over the wall.

He almost fell off when he saw what it was.
It was an amazing sight.
It wasn't a gang of thieves breaking into
   the supermarket.
It was far more unbelievable.
He stood on top of the dustbin quite speechless.
After several minutes he clapped his hands.
The roaring noise stopped.
'Wait there, mate, I want to have
   a word with you,' yelled the policeman.

He climbed down and walked to the car park gate.
A grey-haired old man was waiting for him.
'Right, mate, what do you think
    you're up to?' said the policeman.
The old man looked down at the ground.
'I'm sorry, officer, I didn't think
    I was doing anything wrong.'
    The policeman laughed.

You've only broken about six laws
   that I can think of right now.'
'But skate-boarding isn't breaking the law,'
   said the old man.
'It is on private property.
   Don't worry, I'm not going to book you.
   But I'll tell you this,
      you didn't half give me a fright.'

31

32

The old man held a skate-board in his arms.
He smiled at the policeman.
'You're the first person ever to have
   seen me do my tricks.
   I'm quite good at it, aren't I?'
The policeman nodded.
'My son has one of them skate-boards.
   But he can't do half the things you do!
   If you don't mind my asking,
      how old are you?'
'I'm seventy-two, seventy-three next month.
   Shall I show you my back wheel turn?'
'Yeah, why not?' said the policeman.

The old man put the skate-board down.
With his right foot he flicked at the ground.
He put all his weight on to the back of the board.
The front wheels came off the ground
   and he made a perfect back wheel turn.
The old man glided back to the policeman.

At that moment they both heard the police car.
'Oh, no! They've sent a car over.
   I should have reported back,'
      said the policeman.
   'They must think something is wrong.
   Look, don't worry. I'll do all the talking.
   But no more demos on the board.
   And don't come back here again.
   This is private property.'

The police car pulled up in front of them.
'Sorry, sarge,' said the policeman.
'I forgot to call back.
Nothing doing here.
Just an old boy out for some fresh air.'
The policemen in the car stared at the old man
and the skate-board at his side.
They looked at one another but said nothing.
The old man picked up the board,
shook hands with the policeman
and walked off.
'You wouldn't think he was seventy-two,
would you, sarge?
It's people like him who make this job
worth doing.'

The stone mystery

The school bell rang.
At once the class started to put away
   their books.
The teacher waited for silence.
'Cross your arms and sit up straight.
   We have a test tomorrow.
   What is it on, Tim O'Brien?'
'We have to learn by heart
   the first twenty verses
      of the Sermon on the Mount,' said Tim.
'That's correct', said the teacher.
   'The girls may leave.'
'It's always the girls first', thought Tim.

At last Tim was on his way home.
It was a beautiful spring evening.
He took a short cut over the fields.
The fields had just been planted.
Tim saw a large flock of birds eating the seeds.
He picked up a stone.
'I'll just scare them away', said Tim to himself.
It wasn't a good throw.
The birds didn't even move.
Tim bent down for another stone.

Then he saw it.
It was half buried by the thick mud.
He kicked at it with his boot.
It was bigger than he thought.
Tim bent down and wiped the mud away.
He gasped.
There were strange marks on the smooth stone.

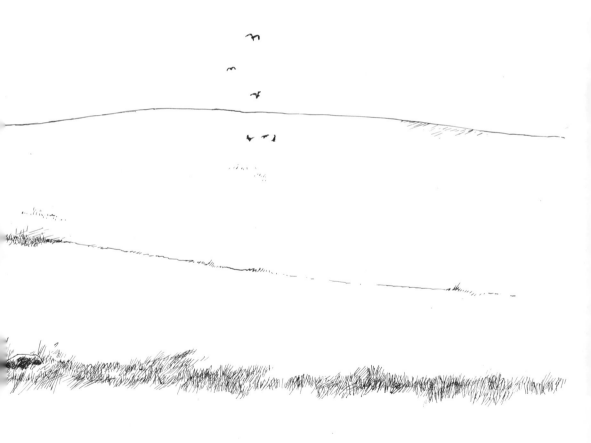

Tim stepped back.
His grandmother had told him
about stones like this.
Stones left by the devil
which brought bad luck.
Stones like these had strange marks on them.
The marks were made by the devil himself.

Tim was eleven years old.
He lived in a small village in Ireland.
He had been taught all about the devil
   and how he tricked people.
It wasn't difficult for him to believe
   that he had found a real devil's stone.

Tim didn't stand looking at the stone
   for very long.
He went straight back to school.
He ran into the classroom.
His teacher was marking a pile of books.
'Well now, what can I do for you, O'Brien?
   You look as though you've seen a ghost.'
The teacher took off his glasses
   and waited for Tim to speak.
'It's worse, sir.
   I've found a devil's stone.'

The teacher listened to Tim's story.
He didn't make fun of the boy.
When Tim had finished,
   the teacher put the books into his bag.
He had heard the same kind of story
   from other villagers.
'All right, O'Brien, let's go
   and have a look at your stone.'

The teacher picked up the stone.
'Most interesting', he said.
   'I don't recognize the writing.
   Can I send this to a friend in Dublin?
   He teaches history at the university.
   I'm sure he can tell us
      how old this stone is
         and what these marks mean.
   Will you let me do this?'
Tim was only too pleased to get rid of the stone.
'Yes, sir, send it to Dublin,' he said.

A few days later, everyone in the village
   was talking about the devil's stone.
Tim's father showed his son a newspaper.
There was a large headline:
   11 YEAR OLD FINDS DEVIL STONE
Tim wasn't sure what to feel.
He was both proud and afraid.
It was fun to see his name in the paper.
But he was afraid the stone would bring
   bad luck to his village.

In Dublin the stone was causing many arguments.
One professor thought it was a Viking stone.
He said the writing was in Old Norse,
   the language spoken by the Vikings.
Another professor said this was nonsense.
He believed the writing was in Hebrew,
   the language spoken by the Jews.
The two professors wrote long essays
   about the stone.
Clearly both men could not be right.

Two months later the mystery was solved.
A young student saw the stone
   on his professor's desk.
The marks were very faint.
They seemed to be impossible to read.
The student took the stone over to the window.
He thought the sunlight would make
   the marks clearer.
He held the stone at arm's length,
   and slowly twisted his wrist.
The student burst out laughing.
Now the marks were easy to read.
'This isn't Hebrew or Old Norse.
   It's written in English!'

At first the professors disagreed with the student.
But soon nearly everyone could read the marks.
It was easy once they knew what to look for
    and how to hold the stone.
The two professors tried to forget the whole thing.
But now they were the joke of Dublin.
Stones started to arrive through the post
    with funny messages for the two wise professors.

You may be wondering what was
    written on the stone.
The words read:

JUNE 1788
AM VERY DRUNK
AGAIN
THIS DAY

Shark!

It was a fine summer's day in Australia.
Thirteen-year-old Ray Short waded into the sea.
It was just right, calm and warm.
He dived under the first wave.

Ray was a good swimmer.
He swam away from the beach,
   and turned on to his back.
He closed his eyes.
He floated like this for about a minute.
As he lay in the water he forgot all about
   school, teachers and homework.

He let himself sink below the waves.
The sea wasn't very clear.
He swam underwater then came up for air.
He was just out of his depth.
Ray kicked to keep himself afloat.
Something touched his leg.
Then he was pulled under.

At first Ray thought someone was playing a joke.
But it wasn't a friend pulling him under.
Ray felt along his side.
His hand touched something hard and rough.
Then he saw the huge mouth
  closed tightly around his leg.

He wanted to scream out.
But he could only say to himself
  the one word, 'shark'.
The shark's dull eyes stared back at the boy.
Ray had been caught by a great white shark.

Ray kicked the shark with his free leg.
But the shark held on.
Ray punched at his eyes.
It still held on.

Ray's head came up above the water.
He gasped a lungful of air.
Then he started waving and shouting.
'Help! Shark! Help! Shark!'

Suddenly the sea was empty of swimmers.
They all rushed to the beach and safety.
Only the boy was left in the water,
    fighting for his life.
Ray heard the shark bell being rung on the beach.

53

Here in Ray's own words is what happened next:
'I tried to swim back to the beach,
   but still couldn't get rid of it.
   I was beginning to panic.
   Then I thought that if I bit it,
      it just might go away.
   I went under and bit it hard on the nose.'

But even this didn't make the shark let go.
Once again Ray's head came out of the water.
He looked towards the beach.
A man was swimming out to him.
'The shark is still here,' cried Ray.
The man didn't seem to hear.
He just kept on swimming towards him.

The life-guard's arms went around Ray's neck.
'Just lie back, boy, I'll do the rest,'
  yelled the life-guard.
'But the shark is still on my leg,' panted Ray.
  'If you don't believe me, look!'
The life-guard smiled.
'Then we'll tow that to the beach as well.'

And that is just what happened.
In the shallow water the shark could be
   clearly seen.
A man started to hit the shark
   with a surf-board.
Somebody else ran up with an oar.
The life-guard grabbed the oar.
He forced it into the shark's mouth.
Gently, Ray's leg was pulled out
   of the teeth-packed mouth.
Ray was rushed to hospital.

A small crowd stood looking at the shark.
'Look at the size of it,' said a man in the crowd.
   'It's over two metres long.
   I'm sure it's a great white.
   Don't go too close.
   It looks dead but you can never tell.'
A small boy pointed to the shark's side.
'It's been badly bitten by another shark.'
'Yeah,' said a girl.
   'It must have been half dead
      when it attacked the swimmer.
   That's why it didn't fight much
      when it was pulled on to the beach.'

Ray quickly got better in hospital.
He can now walk without a stick.
But the teeth marks on his leg remain.
They will always remind him
   of those terrible moments in the sea.
Ray Short is one of the few people
   who has lived to describe a great white attack.

The bare facts

Katie was very nervous.
It was her first day at the big house.
She knocked at the servants' door.
It swung slowly open.
'Yes?' said an old woman.
'I'm the new maid,' said Katie.
'You must always call me ma'am.
I'm Mrs. Perkins, the housekeeper.
Don't stand there letting in the cold.
Come in, and close the door behind you!
Give me your coat,' said Mrs. Perkins.

The old housekeeper stared at Katie.
Katie looked down at the floor.
'You aren't very big.
   How old are you?' asked Mrs Perkins.
'Thirteen, ma'am,' said Katie.

60

Mrs Perkins showed Katie round the house.
It was a long walk.
Katie lost count of the rooms.
There were paintings, vases, tables
   and more paintings.
Katie felt miserable.
She knew they all had to be cleaned.
There wasn't a speck of dust in the house.

'This is the main guest room.
   This is Sara.
   She's the upstairs maid.
   I want you to work with her today.
   She will tell you what to do.'
Mrs. Perkins left Katie with Sara.
Five minutes later
   Katie was on her hands and knees.
She was cleaning out the fire-place.

'Here, mind out!' said Sara.
   'You're getting ash on the carpet.
   Haven't you ever done this before?
   I always get the new girls.'

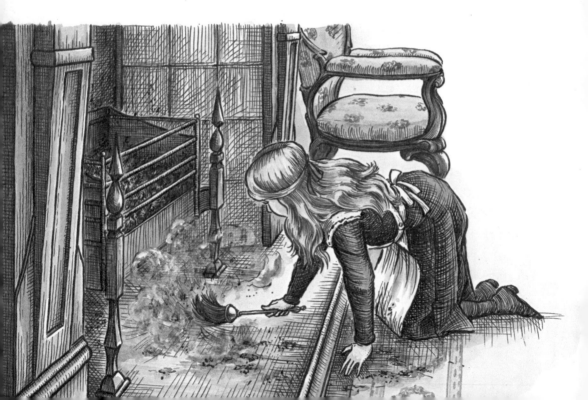

Katie said nothing.
She went on with the job.
Then she heard a bell.
It was ringing in the next room.
Katie stood up.
'Where do you think you're going?' asked Sara.
'I heard a bell,' said Katie.
  'It's still ringing now.
  It's just outside the door.'

Sara started laughing.
'You stay here.
    Bells in this house mean don't move.
    Didn't Mrs. Perkins tell you?'
Katie shook her head.
Mrs. Perkins hadn't said anything about bells.
She went on cleaning.
Katie heard the bell again.
She looked at Sara.

Sara went on making the bed.
Katie didn't understand.
Why didn't anyone answer the bell?
Then she heard footsteps.
Somebody was walking outside.
The ringing and the footsteps went together.
Sara didn't seem to notice.

The footsteps went away.
Katie felt better.
She finished the fire-place.
She dusted the tables and chairs
   and polished the mirror.
The hours went slowly by.

Mrs. Perkins returned.
She looked at Katie's work.
'Not bad for a beginner.
   Tidy yourself up.
   Lady Wallscourt wants to speak to you.
   She likes to see the new girls.
   She'll have a few questions.
   Just answer "Yes, my lady" or "No, my lady".
   Follow me,' said Mrs. Perkins.

Katie wiped her hands on her apron.
Once again they walked through room after room.
Mrs. Perkins stopped and knocked at a door.
'Come in,' said a voice from inside.
Katie followed Mrs. Perkins into the room.
Lady Wallscourt was having her morning tea.
Katie stood beside Mrs. Perkins.
She didn't know what to do with her hands.
At last Lady Wallscourt started to speak.

'I hope you will enjoy working here.'

'Thank you ma'am, I mean my lady,' said Katie.

'Mrs. Perkins has worked here for thirty years.

   I just have one thing to say.

   You may hear a bell upstairs.

   You must never go near that ringing.

   You must never tell anyone about the bell.

   Anyone outside the house, I mean.

   Do you understand me?' asked Lady Wallscourt.

'Yes, my lady.'

'Very well, you may go now.'

Lady Wallscourt poured herself another cup of tea.

68

Once again Katie followed Mrs. Perkins.
Katie knew the way.
But she stayed behind the housekeeper.
They went to the kitchen.
'Sit down,' said Mrs Perkins.
   'I think you might have some questions.
   I'll try to answer them.'

Katie took a deep breath.
'It's not just the bell.
   It's the footsteps.
   There's somebody walking about upstairs.
   Please ma'am, what does it all mean?'

Mrs Perkins sighed.
She looked into Katie's eyes.
Then she started to speak.
'It's Lord Wallscourt.
   He's been like this for a long time.
   You see, my dear, he doesn't like clothes.'
Katie's mouth fell open.
'He doesn't like clothes!
   You mean he doesn't wear any?'

Mrs Perkins looked up at the ceiling.
'Yes, he's up there now.

He's walking around
   as naked as a new born child.
Well that's not quite true.
He does wear something.
He wears a bell round his neck.
It's so we know where he is.
He's a charming old man.
He's quite happy, as long as he's naked.'

Katie worked for Lord and Lady Wallscourt
  for many years.
She eventually became their housekeeper.
She heard the bell nearly every day.
She only saw Lord Wallscourt twice.
Once when he was ill in bed.
And once when he popped his head round the door.

The great British breakfast

Here is a word you know well: *breakfast*.
Say it to yourself.
Now look carefully at the word.
It is made up of two words.
You know both these words: *break* and *fast*.
Many hundreds of years ago the word breakfast
   was two separate words.
People used to say break fast.

Let me try to explain what these two words
   meant all those years ago.
Break is another word for stop.
Fast doesn't only mean quick.
It also means to go without food for a long time.

Let's put the words together.
To break fast means
   to stop going without food.
Now here's an easy question.
When do you eat breakfast?
It's always the first meal of the day.
You haven't eaten since the day before.
So you are breaking a fast.

You've eaten breakfast at least
   two thousand times.
That sounds a lot, but I've eaten
   over eleven thousand breakfasts.
See if you can find out how many breakfasts
   your teacher has eaten.
It may be a difficult sum.
Here is how you do it.
Ask your teacher how old she or he is.
Take off one year because
   small babies don't really have breakfast.
You know there are three hundred
   and sixty-five days in a year.
So three hundred and sixty-five times the age
   of your teacher, less one year,
      will tell you how many breakfasts
         your teacher has eaten.
Just think of all those eggs, plates of cornflakes
   and cups of tea.
All that food would fill your classroom.

Here is my favourite breakfast.
First a glass of grapefruit juice.
Then a boiled egg with the white hard
    and the yolk runny.
Bread and butter cut into soldiers
    to dip into the yolk of the egg.
(The yolk always runs over the edge.)
Next a really hot cup of tea.

If it's Sunday the breakfast
   is only half finished.
Now comes the main course.
A plate covered with bacon, mushrooms,
   one sausage and lots of baked beans.
Another cup of tea.
Finally, two slices of toast
   with butter and marmalade.
What's your favourite breakfast?

Our British breakfast uses food
   from all over the world.
Josh Samson lives in Trinidad
   in the West Indies.
Josh is seventeen years old.
He works with his father in the docks
   for most of the year.
In the summer he helps cut sugar cane.
The work is very hard but Josh
   doesn't earn very much money.
The sugar cane is sent to Britain.
Here it is made into the white sugar
   you put in your tea and on to
      your cornflakes.

Where do your cornflakes come from?
I know your mum buys them
    from the supermarket.
But where are they grown?
Of course cornflakes don't grow on bushes.
They are made from corn.
But where does the corn grow?

Nearly all our cornflakes come
    from the United States.
In the middle of the United States
    are the largest farms in the world.
The flat lands are used to grow
    thousands of square miles of corn.
One field in the corn lands is bigger
    than most English farms.
Chip Walters lives in the corn lands.
He works on his father's farm.

Chip is a motor mechanic.
He makes sure that his father's tractors
   and harvesters never break down.
Chip and his father often have rows.
Mr. Walters wants his son to take over his farm.
Chip doesn't want to do this.
He wants to become a racing driver.

Indra Bedi is thirteen years old.
She lives in the north of India.
She works with her sister on a tea plantation.
Indra's job is to pick the top leaves
   from the tea plants.
She carries a huge basket on her back.
Indra has to fill this several times a day
   with the leaves.
She lives with her family on a small farm.
Her father tries to grow enough food
   to feed his large family.
In a few years, Indra's father will choose
   a husband for his daughter.
Indra is trying to save a little money
   to pay for her wedding.

Without Indra you wouldn't have your
   morning cup of tea.
Josh helps to make that tea taste sweet.
But somebody else is needed.
That somebody is Bill James.

Bill lives in Devon.
He's a cowman.
It's his job to milk forty cows.
He wakes up when it's still dark.
Twice on every day of the year he has
    to take the cows to the milking sheds.
Some of the milk is used to make
    cheese and butter.
Most is taken away by road tankers.

You may have drunk some of Bill's milk.
'I used to work in a factory,' said Bill.
   'The money was good
      and the hours were shorter.
   But I'm not going to work indoors again.
   As a cowman I'm my own boss.
   The farmer pays my wages but he leaves me
      to get on with the job.'

Bill works on Mr Pengallon's farm.
Mr Pengallon is a busy man.
He doesn't only have cows on his farm.
He keeps pigs and chickens as well.
'Farming has changed since I was a boy.
   Our chickens are kept in cages all their lives.
   Even the pigs are kept inside
      for most of the year.
   Nearly all my work is done in my office.
   I only hope people don't stop eating
      eggs and bacon for breakfast.
   You could say my farm is a breakfast farm.'

Do you remember my favourite breakfast?
See if you can find out where my marmalade
  and my baked beans come from.
You will need to read the label
  on a marmalade jar and a baked bean tin.
In small writing there is a list of what's inside.
Try to find out where all the things inside
  are grown.

The treasure of Gilling Beck

'Gary, don't forget your raincoat.'
'Oh, mum, it won't rain today.'
'You're not going tadpoling without your coat.'
Gary held out his arms.
His mother helped him into his coat.
'Don't come back covered with mud.
  And make sure you're home by tea-time.
  Enjoy yourself!'

Gary ran down the street.
He thought about mothers.
Why do they worry so much?
He wasn't a little kid any more.
After all, he would be ten soon.
He climbed over a rusty wire fence.
He made sure it didn't catch on his coat.
He slid down the muddy bank to the stream.
Then he pulled off his shoes and socks
    and rolled up his jeans.

The water wasn't very deep
  but it was icy cold.
Gary stood very still
  as he looked into the stream.
He held his tadpole net just above the surface.
He knew it was no good splashing around.
So he moved the net slowly through the water.
He lifted out the net and looked at his catch.

Nothing, just a few bits of twig
    and lots of weed.
After twenty minutes he had caught
    three lolly sticks, two bottle tops
        and one tadpole.
It was going to be one of those days.
Gary sat by the stream
    and threw stones at a log.

Each stone was a bomb.
The log was a German battleship.
The first bomb went too far.
The second splashed the battleship.
The third bomb was a hit.
The battleship turned slowly over in the water.

Then he saw something
   sticking up out of the mud
      at the edge of the stream.
It was made of metal.
'It looks like the handle of a sword,'
   thought Gary.
First he wiped away the thick mud.
Then he pulled with both hands.
The mud made a strange, sucking noise.
Gary pulled harder.
Out it came!
It was almost a metre long.

'It *is* a sword,' shouted Gary.
   'It's a knight's sword.
   It must be hundreds of years old.'

Gary threw the tadpole back into the stream.
He rolled down his jeans,
   and pulled on his socks and shoes.
It wasn't easy climbing the wire fence
   with the sword and the net in his arms.
He was in such a hurry he almost ripped his coat.

'You're early, Gary.
  No luck today?' asked his mother.
'No taddies, mum, but look at this,' said Gary.
'What have you got there?' she asked.
  'It's dripping all over the carpet.'
'Just look at it, mum,' said Gary.
  'It's a knight's sword.
  I found it near Gilling Beck.
  Look at the handle.'
'Good gracious!' said Gary's mother.
  'I wonder if you're right?
  The handle is very beautiful.
  Bring it into the bathroom.
  I'll wash the mud away.'

When Mr Fridd came home tea wasn't ready.
He found his wife and son
    cleaning a sword in the bathroom.
Soon he had forgotten all about tea.
He was just as excited as Gary.
'I'll show the sword to Auntie Doris.
    She'll know where to take it.
    It might be very old
        and worth a lot of money,' said Mr Fridd.

Auntie Doris went to the Bowes Museum
   in Barnard Castle.
The experts in the museum were amazed
   when they saw the sword.
They thought it was
   probably a thousand years old.
It must have belonged
   to an Anglo-Saxon king or chief.
The experts had seen only one or two swords
   like the one found by Gary.
They told Auntie Doris that it was worth
   a great deal of money.

Life became very busy for Gary.
The telephone never stopped ringing.
Reporters wanted to speak to him.
They wanted to take pictures
    of Gary holding the sword.
BBC television asked Gary to come to London
    to show the sword on *Blue Peter*.

Life was also busy for Mr. and Mrs. Fridd.
They had to talk to a lawyer.
He told them about the law on finding treasure.
It was not a simple law.
'You see, we will have to prove
    that the sword was *lost*,' he explained.
  'If it was *put* there by somebody
      then it belongs to the Queen.
  But I think that we can show
      that it was lost near Gilling Beck.
  It was covered by mud from the stream.
  There it probably stayed until
      Gary found it, one thousand years later.
  If the judge agrees, the sword belongs to Gary.
  Then he can keep it or sell it.'

A judge listened to Gary's story.
He wanted to know where the sword was found.
He wanted to know many things.
But after lots of questions
   he said that the sword *was* Gary's.
It hadn't been hidden.
It didn't belong to the Queen.

Gary sold the sword in London in April 1977.
It was bought by the York Museum for £10,000.
Gary was amazed at the price.
He went to the York Museum
   and saw a photo of himself
     holding the sword.
The sword looked very beautiful
   in its glass case.
Gary felt very proud.

Mrs Fridd has become very interested
   in the history of the sword.
She has her own idea about how it was lost.
The street where she lives has an odd name.
It is called Anteforth Street.
She has found out that Anteforth
   is the name of an Anglo-Saxon battle.
Mrs. Fridd thinks that the sword
   was lost during the battle
     by a Saxon knight, or even a king.

On the next page is an Anglo-Saxon warrior.
Until recently we didn't know very much
    about the Anglo-Saxons who lived in England
        one thousand years ago.
In 1939 an Anglo-Saxon grave
        was opened at Sutton Hoo.
The grave contained a ship thirty metres long.
In the ship were the weapons of a King.
There was also gold jewellery, coins
    and many other priceless objects.

The drawing of the warrior
    is based on the weapons found in Sutton Hoo.
This sword is like the one Gary Fridd found
    in Gilling Beck.
Each man had to fight alongside his chief.
It was the duty of every soldier
    to remain with his chief,
        even if his chief was killed
            and the battle lost.
The poorest soldiers fought
    with a shield and a lance.
The richer warriors had swords
    and wore iron helmets.
Swords were carefully decorated.
They were often handed down
    from father to son.
The Anglo-Saxons believed
    that as a sword grew older
        its power became greater.

Captive audience

The zoo is just about to close.
The zoo-keepers are showing
  the last visitors to the exit.
The gates are locked five minutes later.
Another busy day at Dublin zoo is over.
But there is still a lot of work to be done.

Every keeper has his own job to do.
One keeper has a very special job.
Every night he has to go to the gorillas' cage.
The gorillas are always waiting for him.
They aren't just waiting for fresh food
  and clean water.
They are waiting for a very different treat.
They are the only animals at the zoo
  that have their own television.

At the back of the cage
  is a large black and white television set.
It has a thick, plastic screen.
The two gorillas sit waiting for the keeper.
They know that once the visitors have left
  they will have their evening of television.

'Telly time!' says the keeper.
   'You're in luck today.
   There's a cowboy film on tonight.'
The keeper switches on the set
   and watches the gorillas settle down
      for an evening's viewing.
They sit very close to the screen.
Sometimes they hold hands.
They often eat a television supper.
When they don't like what they see
   they throw their supper at the screen.

Then they turn away and wait
    for their favourite programmes.
Cowboy films are very popular.
The gorillas join in the gun fights.
They punch the plastic screen,
    beat their chests and scream out loud.

'I think they do follow the story,'
  says their keeper.
  'They enjoy all the action shows.
  They always watch the animal programmes.
  And you should see them
    when there's wrestling on.
  That's their real favourite.
  That's why we have the plastic screen.
  They really do punch it hard.'
In the wild, gorillas live in large families.
There's always something to look at or do.
They feel happy and relaxed.
But in the zoo it is different.
Gorillas are clever animals.
They seem to understand that they are prisoners
  in their cages.
During the day it is not so bad.
Visitors are always making fools of themselves.
Some beat their chests at the gorillas.
Others make strange Tarzan noises.
The visitors are quite entertaining.
But at night the gorillas become bored.
Sometimes they pace their cages
  and attack the bars.

Dublin Zoo wasn't the first zoo
   to give their gorillas a television.
The idea came from America.
Somebody in an American zoo
   thought of a way to stop his gorillas
      from becoming bored.
He gave them a T V set.
The gorillas quickly became fans.

In Dublin, the first television set
   didn't last very long in the gorillas' cage.
'They enjoyed it too much!'
   says their keeper.
   'Televisions aren't built to be thumped
      by fully-grown gorillas.
   So we put up a plastic screen.
   Now they can attack the screen
      as much as they like.
   And we have two much happier animals.
   Other animals in the zoo enjoy listening to music.
   But only the gorillas seem to like television.'

The children's crusade

It was a warm May day in France
   in the year 1212.
The streets of Saint Denis were crowded.
The people were waiting to see their King.
There was a loud trumpet blast.
As the doors of the church swung open,
   the crowd pushed forward.

First came the King's bodyguard.
Next came the Bishop of Saint Denis.
A priest holding a large cross
   led out a line of singing choir boys.
As the cross was carried past,
   the crowd dropped to their knees.

They stayed on their knees
    as King Philip walked out of the church.
He walked under a large, golden cloth
    carried by four servants.
In front of the King walked another priest
    who flicked the ground with holy water.
Behind the King marched more of his bodyguard.
Each guard carried a long pike.
They stared into the crowd,
    daring anyone to come too close.

Suddenly there was a shout.
A thin, dirty boy was calling out to the King.
King Philip turned his head.
Three of the bodyguard moved into the crowd.
The King held up his right hand
    to stop the guards.
'Let the boy approach,' he said.

The boy came up to the King,
  bowed and kissed the royal ring.
'Speak boy.
  What is so important?
  Why do you risk your life
    to speak to your King?'
The boy looked into the King's eyes
  and said nothing.
He simply held out a piece of paper.

A priest grabbed the creased paper.
'It's a letter, Your Majesty,' said the priest.
'Read it, then,' said King Philip.
The priest looked at the letter.
His face went white with anger.
'Well, what does it say?' asked King Philip.
'It commands Your Majesty
    to lead an army into the Holy Land.
    This boy is *ordering* you
        to make a Holy War against the Moors!'

King Philip smiled.
'What is your name?' he asked the boy.
'Stephen, Your Majesty.'
'Did you write this?' asked the King.
'No, Your Majesty.
    I was looking after my sheep
        when an angel appeared.
    The letter was given to me by the angel.
    The angel told me to tell the good news.
    God will protect those who fight for Him.'

The King smiled again.

'You are a shepherd,' he said.

'I too am a shepherd.

A shepherd to the people of France.

Boy, return to your sheep.

You have given me the angel's message.'

'You will lead a crusade?' asked Stephen.

'How dare you question your King,'

shouted the priest.

'There will be no crusade.

Return to your fields and your work.'

The priest threw the letter at the boy's feet.

King Philip turned away.

Stephen picked up the letter
  and moved after the King.
A soldier pushed him
  with the wooden end of his pike.
The crowd pointed and laughed at the boy.
Stephen carefully folded the letter
  and placed it inside his shirt.
He walked to the church steps.
Holding his head high, he spoke to the crowd.
'The King will not listen to the angel's message.
  The men of France will not fight.
  I am only twelve years old
    but I will obey God's command.'
'You're mad!' yelled a man.

'What will you do?' shouted another.
  'Walk across the sea
    and fight with your bare hands?'
The crowd walked away.

Stephen did not give up.
He went from town to town.
Everywhere he made the same speech.
The adults ignored him.
But the children of France listened.
Soon there were thousands of children
  following Stephen.

119

The 'Children's Crusade' had begun.
In every town they visited,
  the children were given food and shelter.
There were now almost thirty thousand of them.
Most of them were even younger than Stephen.
Several priests joined the children's army.
They helped Stephen to make his plans.

After weeks of marching, they came
  to a French port.
Some of the children believed
  that the seas would part.
Then they could walk to the Holy Land.
But the seas did not part.
The children had no money to pay for ships.
It seemed that the crusade was over.

Then two rich merchants spoke to Stephen.
'We want to help you,' said the taller merchant.
  'We have a fleet of ships.
  We can take your army to the Holy Land.'
Stephen looked at the two merchants.
One was a black-bearded giant of a man.
His name was Hugh the Iron.
The other was the ugliest man
  the boy had ever seen.
He was known as William the Pig.

'Thank you for your offer,' said Stephen.
  'But we have no money.'
'Money, who said anything about money?
  We want to help you defeat the Moors.
  We ask for nothing in return,' said William.
'When can we leave?' asked Stephen.
'As soon as you are ready,' said Hugh.
'Thank you,' said Stephen.
  'You will always be remembered for this act.'

There were only seven ships.
Thousands of children had to be left behind.
From the shore they watched sadly
  as the fleet set sail.
Then they began the long walk home.
They didn't know it,
  but they were the lucky ones.

The news of Stephen's crusade
  spread across Europe.
In Germany a boy named Nicholas
  heard the news.
If the children of France could go,
  why not the children of Germany?
He repeated Stephen's message.
Children were needed to fight the Holy War.
Once again, an army was formed.
They marched southwards.
The mountains of the Alps lay in their path.
Hundreds died in the terrible climb.
When they reached Italy, many were very sick.
In the port of Genoa no ships would take them.
Nicholas led the children on to Rome.
He thought the Pope would help.
After all, the Pope had called for a crusade
  time and time again.

On the long road to Rome many children
    refused to go on.
They decided to make Italy their new home.
At last, Nicholas and his army
    made camp just outside Rome.
A horseman rode out to meet them.
He had a message from Pope Innocent.
'His Holiness asks you to come into Rome.
    He wants to thank you
        and give you his blessing.'

The children were very excited.
Tomorrow they would see the Pope.
For the first time, things
    seemed to be getting better.
The children sang round their camp fires.
Nicholas went from group to group.
He felt sad.
They all looked so thin and tired.
He tried to hide his thoughts from the others.

The march into Rome started at first light.
All along the road were vast crowds.
They gave the children flowers and food.
Nicholas rode a horse at the head of his army.
As they passed each church, the bells were rung.
When they came to the church of Saint Peter's,
    Nicholas climbed down off his horse.
He knelt and kissed the ground.
The Pope was waiting for them.
There were tears in the old man's eyes.
He blessed the children.
Then he made a long speech.
A priest repeated his words in German.
The Pope thanked them.
They had shown great love for God.
But they were not to go on.
He wanted them to return to Germany.
They must wait until they were older.
Children were not meant to fight.

Just a few hundred of the children
    tried to cross the Alps again.

Only a handful ever reached their homes.
Nobody knows what happened to Nicholas.
Twenty years later came news
    of the French children.
One ship had sunk in a storm.
The other six ships had been caught by pirates.

The story of the Children's Crusade
    was told and retold.
Over hundreds of years
    it was changed many times.
In Germany the story became a fairy tale
    about a small village in the mountains.

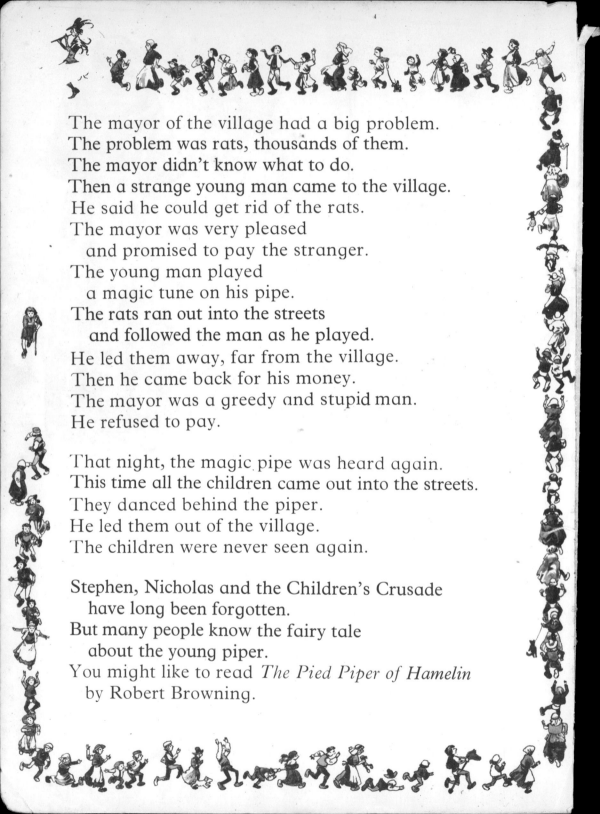

The mayor of the village had a big problem.
The problem was rats, thousands of them.
The mayor didn't know what to do.
Then a strange young man came to the village.
He said he could get rid of the rats.
The mayor was very pleased
    and promised to pay the stranger.
The young man played
    a magic tune on his pipe.
The rats ran out into the streets
    and followed the man as he played.
He led them away, far from the village.
Then he came back for his money.
The mayor was a greedy and stupid man.
He refused to pay.

That night, the magic pipe was heard again.
This time all the children came out into the streets.
They danced behind the piper.
He led them out of the village.
The children were never seen again.

Stephen, Nicholas and the Children's Crusade
    have long been forgotten.
But many people know the fairy tale
    about the young piper.
You might like to read *The Pied Piper of Hamelin*
    by Robert Browning.